Bearded Dragon

A Fun and Educational Book for Kids with Amazing Facts and Pictures

Table of Contents

Table of Contents..3

Introduction 5

Scientific Name...7

Appearance 9

Geography 11

Behavior..13

Reproduction 16

Social Life..19

Habitat 21

Senses..24

Feeding 27

Diet...30

Babies...33

Predators..36

Evolution..39

Population 42

Conservation Status 45

Health 48

Lifespan 51

Conclusion 53

Introduction

Australia's arid regions are home to a species of lizard known as the bearded dragon, or Pogona. They make popular pets because of their amiable dispositions, simplicity of maintenance, and attractive appearance. The spiny protrusions under their chin, which can swell when they feel threatened or angry and give the appearance of a beard, are what give bearded dragons its name.

Agamidae is the family of reptiles that includes bearded dragons. With the right care, they can reach a length of two feet and have a lifespan of up to 15 years. They consume a range of fruits, vegetables, and insects because they are omnivores. Bearded dragons are superb climbers and sunbathers, and they need a warm, dry habitat to thrive.

Due to their well-known placid demeanor, bearded dragons make excellent pets for both novice and seasoned reptile keepers. Bearded dragons can grow loving and like being held with the right handling and care. They are intriguing to observe and engage with since they are interested and active.

Scientific Name

Pogona vitticeps is the bearded dragon's scientific name.

Appearance

Bearded dragons are easily recognized thanks to their striking appearance. They have a strong body, a triangular-shaped head, and broad, triangular spines that run the length of their back. Little, sharp scales that cover their skin come in a variety of hues according on the age and gender of the animal.

Bearded dragon adults can grow to be 16 to 24 inches long and weigh anywhere from 350 to 600 grams. They use their long, powerful tails for communication and balance. The spiny outgrowth under their chin, which can blow out when they feel threatened or wish to show hostility, is their most distinguishing characteristic.

Large, spherical eyes with a broad field of vision and the ability to see in both color and black and white are another feature of bearded dragons. Moreover, they have independent eye movement, which enables them to keep an eye out for prospective predators and prey. Generally, bearded dragons are a popular choice for pets because of their distinctive and stunning appearance.

Geography

The central and eastern portions of Australia are home to bearded dragons, which are native to the dry regions of that continent. They can be found in the bushland and woodland parts of the Northern Territory, Queensland, and New South Wales, but they are most frequently seen in the desert portions of these states.

Bearded dragons can survive in temperatures as high as 105°F and are well-adapted to the harsh, desert climate of Australia. Moreover, they can be found in a range of environments, such as rocky outcrops, spinifex grasslands, and wooded places.

Bearded dragons have been brought to various parts of the world due to their popularity as pets, including the United States, Europe, and Asia, where they are now kept as pets and occasionally bred in captivity. They are regarded as an invasive species in these regions, though, and they could endanger local fauna.

Behavior

Bearded dragons are popular pets because of their well-known placid and peaceful demeanor. They are nocturnal, which means they sleep at night and are most active during the day. They can be maintained in pairs or small groups because they are social animals, but they shouldn't be kept alongside other species.

Bearded dragons are also clever creatures that can recognize and respond to their owners by name. They even want to be handled and petted. They enjoy climbing, exploring their environment, and soaking up the sun because they are naturally curious creatures.

The capacity to "beard," or puff out the spiky outgrowth beneath their chin to appear larger and more frightening, is one of the most distinguishing habits of bearded dragons. When they feel threatened or afraid, this behavior is frequently observed.

Bearded dragons can also express hostility or submission by their body language, which includes head nodding, waving of the arms, and raising of the tail. In order to communicate with others, they may also emit a range of noises, such as hissing, chirping, and even sneezing.

Overall, bearded dragons are fascinating and engaging creatures with a distinctive range of traits that make them cherished household pets.

Reproduction

Male and female bearded dragons differ physically due to the sexual dimorphism of the species. Female bearded dragons tend to be smaller and have less pronounced underbelly spikes than males, who also tend to be larger overall.

In the spring, when the males of bearded dragons grow more aggressive and territorial, mating often takes place. The male will grab the female from behind and hold onto her with his spiny hind legs while mating takes place.

Each clutch of eggs that a female bearded dragon lays after mating normally contains between 10 and 30 eggs, depending on the size of the female. This happens two to three times each year on average. Typically, the female excavates a shallow hole in sandy soil or another suitable substrate, and then lays her eggs there.

The time needed for bearded dragon eggs to hatch can range from 50 to 70 days, depending on the temperature and humidity of the incubation environment. Baby bearded dragons are about 3 inches long when they hatch, and they need constant attention and nutrition to grow into healthy adults.

It is generally advised that experienced breeders rather than novices handle bearded dragon breeding because it takes specific knowledge and care.

Social Life

Bearded dragons are social creatures that can be kept in couples or small groups, but it's crucial to introduce them to one another slowly and carefully observe how they interact. During the breeding season, when males battle for females and create dominance hierarchies, bearded dragons are known to congregate in huge groups in the wild.

Bearded dragons can exhibit a variety of social activities when kept in captivity, such as sharing food and resting areas, grooming one another, and even cuddling. To avoid antagonism and competitiveness, it's crucial to give every individual ample room and resources.

Bearded dragons can develop close relationships with their owners and may take pleasure in routine handling and interaction. Since they are clever creatures, they may be trained to recognize their owners and obey their directions.

Bearded dragons, in general, are gregarious creatures that may prosper in a variety of social settings as long as they are given the proper care and resources to fulfill their emotional and physical needs.

Habitat

Native to Australia's dry regions, bearded dragons can be found there in a variety of habitats, including grasslands, deserts, and wooded areas. Bearded dragons in captivity need a home that resembles their natural habitat and gives them the room and resources they need to thrive.

A terrarium or vivarium that is at least 40 gallons in size and with a screened top to allow for optimum ventilation is the best environment for a bearded dragon. The enclosure needs to include numerous hiding spots, including rocks, logs, and plants, and it needs to be lined with an appropriate substrate, like reptile carpet or sand.

A heat source, such as a ceramic heater or basking lamp, is also necessary for bearded dragon enclosures to maintain a temperature gradient for the animals. The temperature during the day should be around 100°F, while at night it should be about 70°F. In order to deliver the necessary UV radiation for calcium absorption and general health, UVB lighting is also crucial.

Bearded dragons need a sufficient habitat as well as a variety of insects, veggies, and fruits to eat as well as access to clean, fresh water. To support their physical and emotional wellbeing, it is crucial to give them the proper hiding places, relaxing areas, and other environmental enrichment.

Ultimately, a bearded dragon kept in captivity needs a well-designed and well-maintained habitat to preserve its health and happiness.

Senses

Bearded dragons have a variety of senses that they employ to explore their surroundings and communicate with other creatures. They have the following senses:

1. Sight: Bearded dragons have keen vision and can distinguish between different colors and motion. The parietal eye, which is a third eye on the top of their heads and is sensitive to light, aids in controlling their circadian rhythms.

2. Hearing: Bearded dragons have keen hearing and are capable of picking up low-frequency sounds like the rumble of approaching predators or the smell of cooking food.

3. Smell: Bearded dragons use their excellent sense of smell to find food and prospective mates. They are able to recognize pheromones in the air because to a particular organ called the Jacobson's organ.

4. Touch: Because of their sensitive skin, bearded dragons are able to sense temperature changes and vibrations. They converse with other animals through touch, for instance, during courtship rituals.

Overall, bearded dragons have highly developed senses that enable them to live in and interact with their natural habitat.

By include climbing structures and hiding spots in their environment, you can help excite their senses and improve their general health and wellbeing.

Feeding

Due to their omnivorous nature, bearded dragons need a diversified diet that contains both insects and plant things. They should be fed both commercial diets and fresh meals while kept in captivity to make sure they get all the nutrients they require to stay healthy.

The following recommendations are for feeding a bearded dragon:

1. Insects: Crickets, mealworms, superworms, and roaches are among the many insects that bearded dragons like to eat. Before giving these insects to the bearded dragon, they should have their guts filled with healthy food. To support optimal bone health, you can also dust the insects with a calcium and vitamin D supplement.

2. Vegetables: Dark leafy greens, squash, carrots, and sweet potatoes should all be included in the diet of bearded dragons. Daily servings of these veggies should be made with little pieces.

3. Fruits: Berry, mango, and melon are just a few examples of the fruit that bearded dragons can be given in tiny amounts. Fruits, however, should only be served in moderation because of their high sugar content.

4. Commercial diets: Bearded dragons can also be fed commercial foods, which is a practical choice. These diets should be supplemented with fresh foods rather than serving as your bearded dragon's primary source of sustenance.

5. Water: Bearded dragons must always have access to fresh water, which should be put out in a shallow dish. Some bearded dragons like drinking from a spray bottle or dropper.

It's crucial to keep an eye on your bearded dragon's food and make any adjustments based on their appetite and general health. Giving them a varied diet and offering suitable environmental enrichment, such as hiding spots and things to climb, can aid in piqueing their interest in food and advance their general health and wellbeing.

Diet

Due to their omnivorous nature, bearded dragons need a diet that is balanced and contains both plant and animal stuff. They consume a variety of insects, plants, and occasionally small animals in the wild. It is crucial to mimic their natural diet in captivity to make sure they get all the nutrients they require.

The following recommendations are for feeding a bearded dragon:

1. Insects: Crickets, mealworms, superworms, and roaches are among the many insects that bearded dragons like to eat. Before giving these insects to the bearded dragon, they should have their guts filled with healthy food. To support optimal bone health, you can also dust the insects with a calcium and vitamin D supplement.

2. Vegetables: Dark leafy greens, squash, carrots, and sweet potatoes should all be included in the diet of bearded dragons. Daily servings of these veggies should be made with little pieces.

3. Fruits: Berry, mango, and melon are just a few examples of the fruit that bearded dragons can be given in tiny amounts.

Fruits, however, should only be served in moderation because of their high sugar content.

4. Commercial diets: Bearded dragons can also be fed commercial foods, which is a practical choice. These diets should be supplemented with fresh foods rather than serving as your bearded dragon's primary source of sustenance.

5. Water: Bearded dragons must always have access to fresh water, which should be put out in a shallow dish. Some bearded dragons like drinking from a spray bottle or dropper.

It's crucial to keep an eye on your bearded dragon's food and make any adjustments based on their appetite and general health. Giving a child too much food can result in obesity and other health issues, so it's crucial to give them the appropriate amount of food for their size and age. Offering suitable environmental enrichment, like as hiding spots and climbable objects, can also aid in promoting their appetite and general health and wellbeing.

Babies

Bearded dragon hatchlings, often known as baby dragons, need special care to ensure a healthy and robust adulthood. The following guidelines should be followed when taking care of young bearded dragons:

Housing is important since young bearded dragons need a smaller space than adults. For a single hatchling, a 20-gallon tank or equivalent sized cage is suitable. The enclosure needs to provide hiding places, a shallow water dish, a UVB light, and a basking area.

2. Temperature: To provide hatchlings the warmth they require to digest their food and control their body temperature, the basking location should be maintained at a temperature of 100-110°F (38-43°C). Maintaining the enclosure's cooler end at about 80°F (27°C) is recommended.

3. Feeding: Little bearded dragons need to be fed more frequently than adults do. Many times every day, they should be given small, appropriate-sized crickets or other insects in addition to freshly sliced vegetables.

4. Supplements: To encourage healthy bone development, hatchlings need calcium and vitamin D3 supplements. A UVB light should be used to deliver vitamin D3 while calcium

powder should be sprinkled on their food many times each week.

5. Handling: It's critical to handle hatchlings carefully and provide appropriate body support. At first, they may be anxious and skittish, but with time and regular treatment, they can develop into tame and sociable pets.

It is crucial to monitor the growth of hatchlings and modify care as necessary since as they grow, their needs will alter. Offering suitable environmental enrichment, like as hiding spots and climbable objects, can also aid in promoting their appetite and general health and wellbeing.

Predators

There are numerous predators of bearded dragons in the wild. They have therefore developed a number of defenses to keep them from being eaten. Their natural predators include, among others:

1. Birds of prey: Raptors like hawks and eagles occasionally hunt bearded dragons.

2. Snakes: Bearded dragons are naturally preyed upon by snakes, especially pythons and venomous species like the brown snake and death adder.

3. Monitor lizards: Bearded dragons have been preyed upon by larger monitor lizards like the perentie and lace monitor.

4. Dingoes and foxes: In Australia, these animals may also hunt bearded dragons.

Bearded dragons have a number of adaptations that help them defend themselves from predators. For instance, they can alter their color to blend in with their surroundings and so make it more difficult for predators to find them. In order to appear bigger and more dangerous to predators, they can also puff up their bodies and expand their jaws widely. They can also run on their rear legs, which makes it possible for them to move fast and avoid danger.

Bearded dragons are normally protected from these predators when they are kept in captivity, but it is still crucial to give them a safe and secure enclosure to stop them from escaping or getting hurt by other pets or wildlife.

Evolution

It is thought that bearded dragons first appeared in Australia in the Oligocene period, some 30 million years ago. They are a member of the family Agamidae, which is home to more than 300 different species of lizards.

Bearded dragons have developed a number of adaptations over millions of years that help them endure in their harsh desert surroundings. In order to avoid predators and control their body temperature, for instance, they can alter their color to blend in with their surroundings. To minimize surface area and water loss, they can flatten their bodies and tuck their legs down close to their torso.

The distinctive throat pouch of bearded dragons, which they utilize to frighten off rivals and possible predators, is another crucial adaptation. Bearded dragons will puff out their throat pouches and open their mouths wide to make themselves appear bigger and more threatening when they feel threatened or while asserting their dominance.

Bearded dragons have evolved various behavioral tactics in addition to these physical adaptations to help them thrive in their environments. They can thermoregulate, for instance, by laying in the sun during the day and seeking cover in colder places at night. They can also endure for extended periods of time without water because they acquire the majority of their moisture from the food they eat.

In general, bearded dragons serve as an illustration of the amazing adaptations that can develop through millions of years of evolution, enabling animals to flourish in even the most difficult habitats.

Population

Due to its vast spread and solitary lifestyle, it is challenging to assess the bearded dragon population in the wild. Nonetheless, some research opine that habitat loss, introduced predators, and other negative effects of humans may be contributing to their populations possibly diminishing.

In captivity, bearded dragons are produced because they are beloved pets. Because of this, captive-bred bearded dragons are very common in the pet trade and are easily found in pet shops and online.

Bearded dragons can make wonderful pets, but in order to survive, they need particular care and attention. Prospective owners should do their study and be ready to offer a sufficient enclosure, an appropriate feed, and veterinary care when necessary because they can live up to 20 years in captivity and grow rather large.

It's also crucial to think about where captive-bred bearded dragons come from. Some breeders utilize unethical or unsustainable methods, like selecting for physical characteristics that can lead to health issues or removing animals from the wild to supplement their breeding population. Bearded dragons should not be purchased from pet stores or other places with questionable breeding procedures; instead, prospective owners should look for reputable breeders who place a high priority on the health and welfare of their animals.

Conservation Status

Depending on the species and area where they are found, bearded dragon conservation status varies. Although some populations of bearded dragons may be in danger owing to habitat loss, introduced predators, and other human-related effects, the majority of bearded dragon species are not generally regarded as threatened or endangered.

The Western Bearded Dragon (Pogona minor minor) is one of the bearded dragon species that the International Union for Conservation of Nature has designated as Vulnerable (IUCN). The populations of this species, which is only found in a small area of Western Australia, have decreased as a result of habitat loss and fragmentation brought on by mining, agriculture, and urban expansion.

Bearded dragons may be affected by climate change in addition to habitat loss, as changing weather patterns and increased temperatures could affect their habitats and food sources.

Generally, the bearded dragon's conservation status emphasizes the need to protect their habitats and minimize human interference in the areas where they are located. The demand for wild-caught animals can also be decreased with the aid of initiatives to encourage ethical captive breeding and pet ownership, which will aid in the preservation of these intriguing and distinctive reptiles.

Health

Health Bearded dragons, like all animals, are prone to a variety of health problems, some of which can be serious or even fatal. Owners must be aware of the symptoms of typical health issues and seek veterinarian care as necessary.

The following are some of the most typical ailments that bearded dragons may experience:

1. Metabolic Bone Disease: This illness, which can result in weakening bones and other health issues, is brought on by a diet lacking in calcium or vitamin D.

2. Impaction: This happens when a bearded dragon consumes a foreign object that is excessively big or indigestible, causing a blockage in the digestive system.

3. Parasites: Internal and external parasites, such as mites, ticks, and intestinal worms, can harm bearded dragons.

4. Respiratory infections: These can result in symptoms including fatigue, lack of appetite, and wheezing and are frequently brought on by bacterial or viral infections.

5. Mouth rot: This bacterial infection of the mouth can cause pus-filled gums and other symptoms, including swollen gums.

By giving their bearded dragons a nutritious, balanced food, a suitable enclosure with the right heating and lighting, and frequent veterinary exams, owners can help prevent these and other health problems. Also, it's critical to handle bearded dragons gently and keep them away from other animals or stressful situations that could impair their immune systems.

Lifespan

Compared to many other reptiles, bearded dragons have a reasonably long lifespan, with individuals lasting up to 10-15 years in the wild and up to 20 years or more in captivity with the right care.

A number of elements, including genetics, diet, environment, and veterinary treatment, can affect a bearded dragon's longevity. Predation, illness, and habitat loss are just a few of the difficulties wild bearded dragons must contend with, all of which can shorten their lives. If given a nutritious, balanced diet, a suitable habitat with the right heating and lighting, and regular veterinary examinations, bearded dragons can live longer in captivity.

Bearded dragon owners must be aware of the possible lifetime of their pets and provide them the care and attention they require in order for them to enjoy long and healthy lives.

Conclusion

The bearded dragon is a fascinating and well-known reptile that is renowned for its distinctive appearance, friendly nature, and relatively long lifespan. Bearded dragons are native to Australia's dry regions, where they are well suited to their surroundings and exhibit a variety of fascinating habits.

Although though the majority of bearded dragon species are not designated vulnerable or endangered, habitat loss and other negative effects of human activity may put some populations in jeopardy. As a result, it's critical to protect their habitats and control human interference in the areas where they are found.

It is crucial for anyone considering keeping a bearded dragon as a pet to learn about its care requirements and to give it the proper enclosure, diet, and veterinarian attention when necessary. Bearded dragons can make fantastic pets for many years to come if given the right attention and care.